MARGARET FULTON BOOK OF QUICK MEALS

MARGARET FULTON'S BOOK OF QUICK MEALS

octopus

CONTENTS

Soups & Starters	6
Main-Course Dishes	24
Vegetables & Salads	50
Snacks & Supper Dishes	64
Desserts	78
Index	94

This edition published in 1989
by Octopus Books Limited,
part of Reed International Books,
Michelin House, 81 Fulham Road,
London SW3 6RB

Copyright © Cathay Books, 1980

Reprinted 1991

ISBN 0 7064 5011 6

Produced by Mandarin Offset
Printed and bound in Hong Kong

INTRODUCTION

The Margaret Fulton Book of Quick Meals is designed especially for those whose time is limited but who, none the less, like to serve delicious food. Accordingly, no recipe in the book should take more than 45 minutes to prepare and cook; many will take far less.

Recipes are provided to suit every occasion and everyone's pocket – from a celebration dinner of fillet steak to a quick cheese snack.

To keep preparation time to a minimum, packaged, canned and frozen foods are used in many recipes. Of course, you are not obliged to take the short cuts – use fresh meat and vegetables rather than canned, if you have the extra time needed to prepare them. Having said that, rest assured that the convenience foods used in these recipes are of such high quality that none of the dishes will suffer because of the very sensible short cuts. On the contrary, your family and friends will be impressed by your culinary expertise and speed!

Margaret Fulton

NOTES

Standard spoon and cup measurements are used in all recipes
1 tablespoon = one 20 ml spoon
1 teaspoon = one 5 ml spoon
All spoon measures are level
1 cup = 250 ml.

Fresh herbs are used unless otherwise stated. If unobtainable substitute a bouquet garni of the equivalent dried herbs, or use dried herbs instead but halve the quantities stated.

Use freshly ground black pepper when pepper is specified.

Ovens should be preheated to the specified temperature.

For all recipes, quantities are given in both metric and imperial measures. Follow either set but not a mixture of both, because they are not inter-changeable.

SOUPS & STARTERS

Spinach Consommé

2 × 411 g cans
  consommé
1 × 425 g can
  spinach purée
¾ cup dry sherry
pepper

Place the consommé, spinach purée and sherry in a pan and heat gently to just below boiling point.

Sprinkle with pepper to taste before serving.

Serves 4 to 6

Georgian Peanut Soup

2 × 283 g cans cream of chicken soup
1/3 cup salted peanuts, finely chopped
2/3 cup cream
1/2 cup dry sherry

Pour the soup into a pan, add the peanuts and heat gently. Do not boil.

When hot, stir in the cream and sherry and heat gently for 2 minutes.

Serve with toasted slices of French bread.

Serves 4

Cream of Pea and Ham Soup

1 × 600 ml packet green pea soup mix
2½ cups milk
2 cups water
125 g (4 oz) cooked ham, finely chopped
60 g (2 oz) frozen peas
2 cups natural low-fat yogurt
pepper

Place the powdered soup mix in a pan and gradually stir in the milk and water. Bring slowly to the boil, stirring constantly, then add the ham and peas. Cover and simmer for 20 minutes, stirring frequently.

Just before serving, stir in the yogurt and pepper to taste. Serve hot with crusty French bread.

Serves 4 to 6

Cream of Carrot Soup

2 × 440 g cans carrots
2 onions, chopped
60 g (2 oz) butter
1 cup fresh white breadcrumbs
2½ cups milk
salt and pepper
chopped parsley to garnish

Put the carrots, with their juice, the onions, butter and breadcrumbs in a saucepan. Add the milk and bring to the boil. Cover and simmer for 5 minutes.

Rub through a sieve or work in an electric blender until smooth. Add salt and pepper to taste.

Reheat gently before serving, garnished with parsley.

Serves 4 to 6

Tomato and Yogurt Soup

2 × 425 g cans tomatoes
2 cloves garlic, chopped
juice of 1 lemon
1 tablespoon sugar
1 tablespoon Worcestershire sauce
2 cups natural low-fat yogurt
salt and pepper

Put the tomatoes, with their juice, the garlic, lemon juice, sugar and Worcestershire sauce in an electric blender and work for about 3 minutes, until smooth.

Stir in the yogurt and add salt and pepper to taste. Chill for at least 4 hours.

Serves 4 to 6

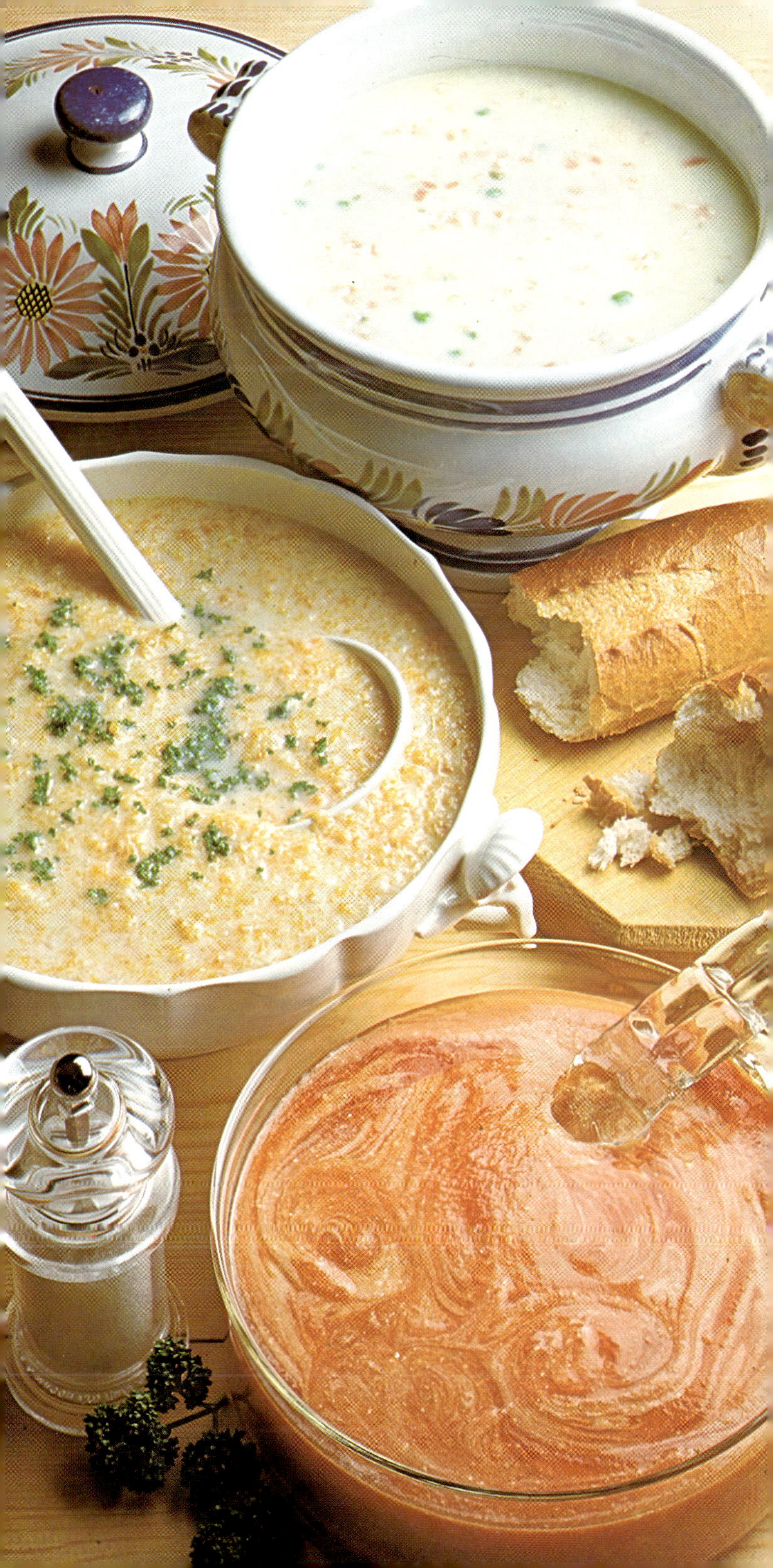

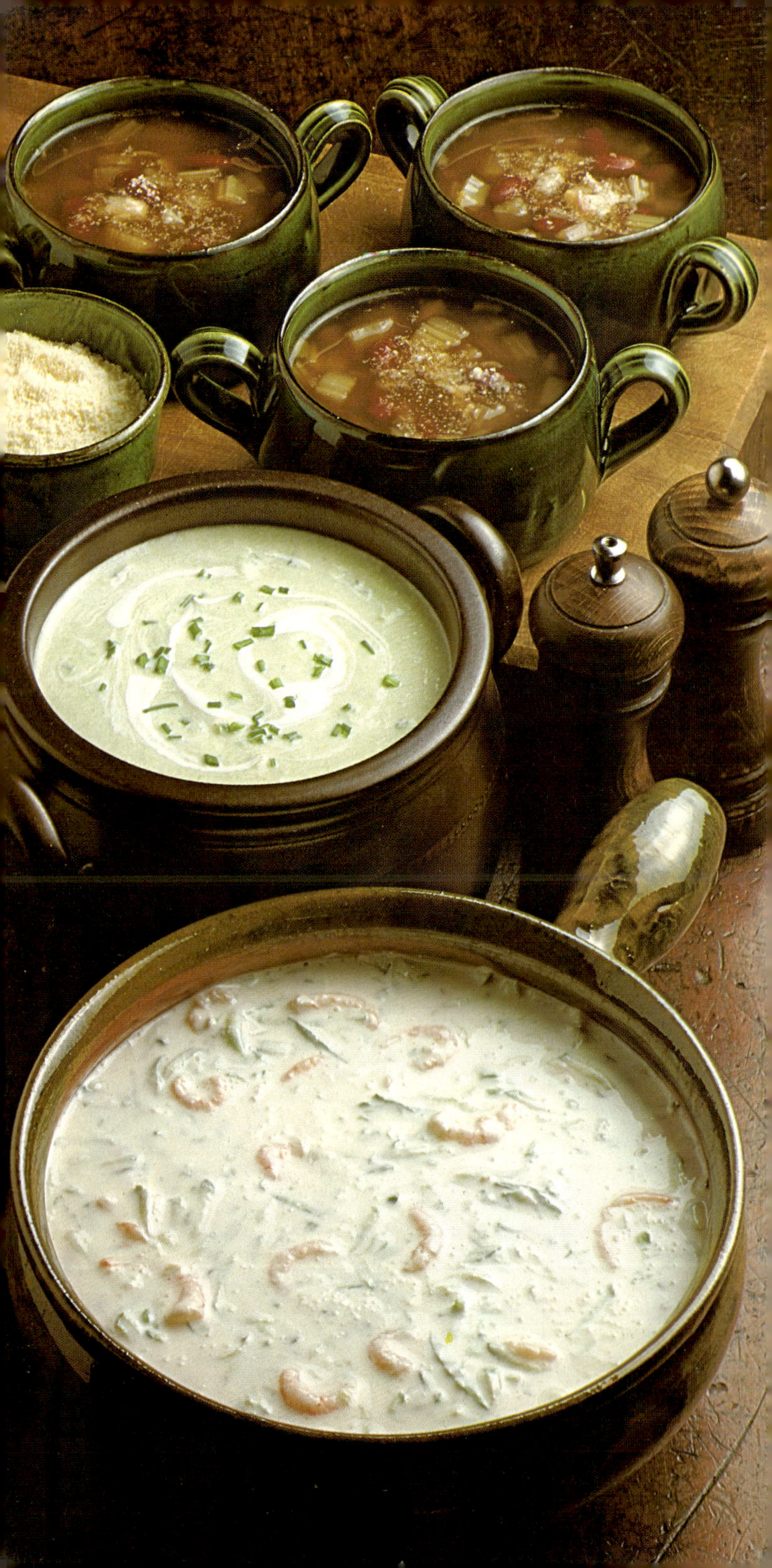

Celery and Onion Soup

1 × 524 g can celery hearts
1 × 440 g can red kidney beans
1 × 425 g can French onion soup
1¼ cups water
½ cup medium sherry
salt and pepper
grated Parmesan cheese to serve

Drain and chop the celery hearts, reserving the liquid. Drain the kidney beans.

Put the onion soup, celery hearts with their liquid, kidney beans, water and sherry in a saucepan. Heat to just below boiling point and add salt and pepper to taste.

Pour into individual soup bowls and sprinkle with Parmesan cheese to serve.
Serves 4 to 6

Vichysoisse

60 g (2 oz) butter
3 small leeks, thinly sliced
1 × 440 g can new potatoes, drained and chopped
3 cups milk
1 cup cream
salt and white pepper
3 tablespoons chopped chives

Melt the butter in a saucepan, add the leeks and cook gently for about 15 minutes until soft.

Put the leeks, potatoes and milk in an electric blender and work until smooth. Stir in the cream and season with salt and pepper to taste. Stir in 2 tablespoons of the chives. Chill for at least 1 hour.

Sprinkle with the remaining chives before serving.
Serves 4

Cucumber and Prawn Soup

1 large cucumber
salt and pepper
1¼ cups natural low-fat yogurt
4 tablespoons lemon juice
1 cup cream
2 tablespoons chopped chives
125 g (4 oz) shelled prawns

Grate the unpeeled cucumber into a bowl and sprinkle lightly with salt. Leave for 15 minutes.

Mix the yogurt, lemon juice and cream together and add to the cucumber. Stir in the chives, prawns and salt and pepper to taste.

Chill the soup for at least 1 hour before serving.
Serves 4

Creamed Mushrooms on Toast

60 g (2 oz) butter
1 small onion, finely chopped
juice of 1 lemon
250 g (8 oz) button mushrooms, sliced
1 tablespoon cornflour
1½ cups cream
2 teaspoons curry paste
salt and pepper
4 slices wholemeal bread, toasted and buttered
chopped parsley to garnish

Melt the butter in a frying pan, add the onion and fry gently until soft. Add the lemon juice and mushrooms and fry gently for 3 minutes.

Stir in the cornflour and cook, stirring, for 2 minutes. Gradually add the cream and cook gently, without boiling, until thickened. Add the curry paste with salt and pepper to taste.

Divide the mixture between the hot toast slices. Garnish with parsley and serve immediately.
Serves 4

Roe-Stuffed Baked Tomatoes

45 g (1½ oz) butter
1 small onion, finely chopped
1 cup fresh white breadcrumbs
1 × 99 g can smoked cod's roe
grated rind of ½ lemon
salt and pepper
cayenne pepper
4 tomatoes, halved, seeded and drained
2-3 tablespoons dry white wine
black olives to garnish

Melt 30 g (1 oz) of the butter in a frying pan, add the onion and fry until soft. Add the breadcrumbs and fry until golden. Keep 4 teaspoons of the mixture on one side.

Break up the cod's roe and stir into the breadcrumb mixture with the lemon rind. Season with salt, pepper and cayenne to taste.

Fill the tomato halves with the cod's roe mixture. Spoon the wine over the filling. Sprinkle with the reserved breadcrumb mixture and dot with the remaining butter.

Cook in a preheated moderate oven, 180°C (350°F), for 15 to 20 minutes until the tomatoes are just tender. Serve hot, garnished with olives.

Serves 4

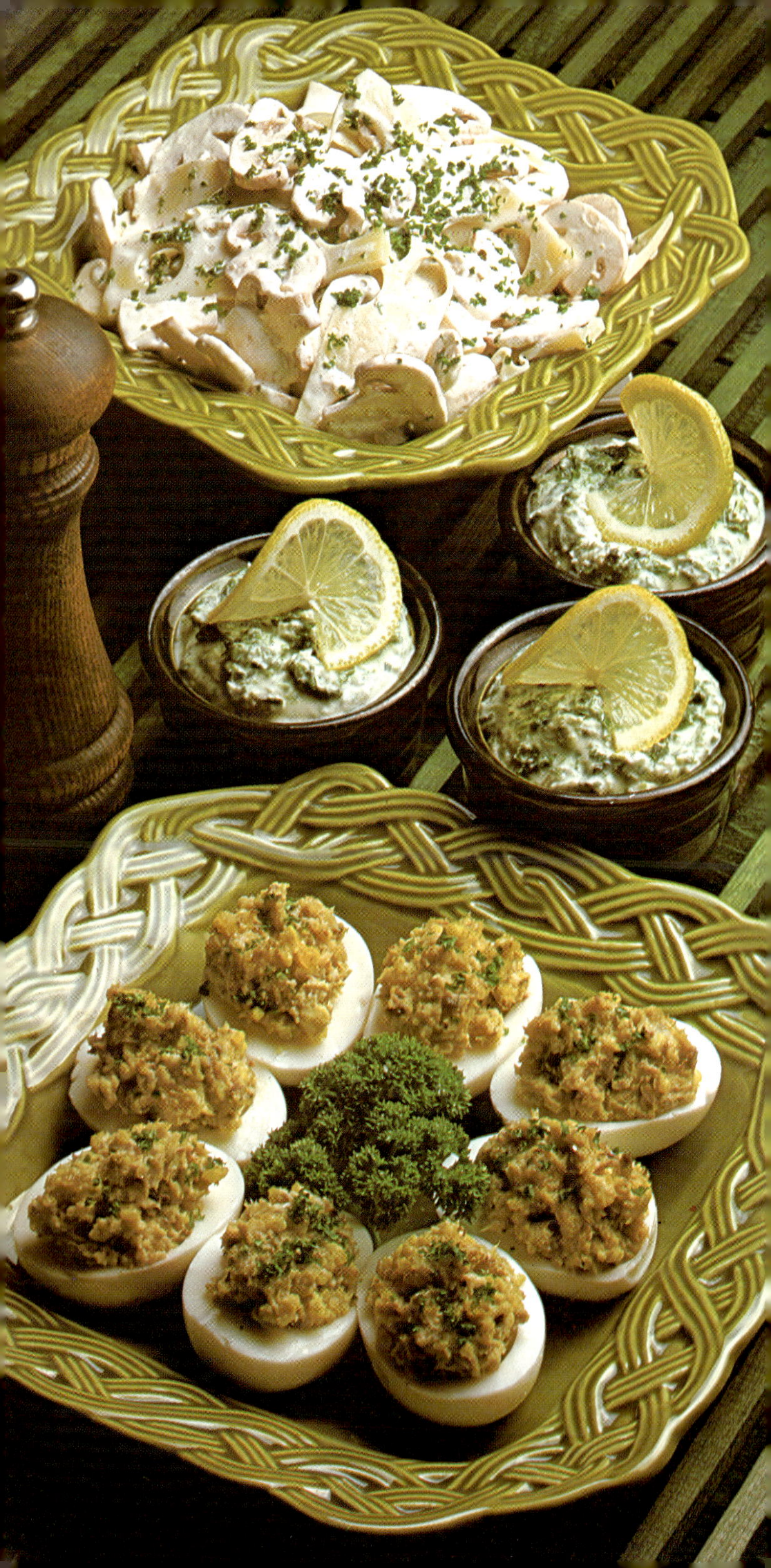

Mushroom and Emmenthal Salad

125 g (4 oz)
  Emmenthal cheese
250 g (8 oz) button
  mushrooms, sliced
1 cup cream
juice of 2 lemons
salt and pepper
chopped parsley to
  garnish

Cut the cheese into thin strips and mix with the mushrooms and cream.
  Add the lemon juice and salt and pepper to taste; toss well.
  Spoon into a serving dish and sprinkle with parsley.
Serves 4

Spinach and Cream Cheese Pâté

250 g (8 oz) cream
  cheese
125 g (4 oz) frozen
  chopped spinach,
  thawed
few drops of Tabasco
  sauce
juice of ½ lemon
grated nutmeg
salt and pepper
4 lemon twists to
  garnish

Beat the cream cheese until soft. Drain the spinach thoroughly, then gradually add to the cream cheese, beating constantly.
  Add the Tabasco, lemon juice and nutmeg, salt and pepper to taste. Continue beating until the pâté is thoroughly blended. Spoon into individual dishes and chill well.
  Garnish each portion with a lemon twist. Serve with buttered wholemeal toast.
Serves 4
NOTE: Cooked fresh, or canned spinach may be used.

Sardine Eggs

4 hard-boiled eggs
1 × 106 g can
  sardines in oil
1 tablespoon fresh
  white breadcrumbs
2 tablespoons
  mayonnaise
1 tablespoon lemon
  juice
salt and pepper
chopped parsley to
  garnish

Cut the eggs in half lengthways and remove the yolks. Drain the sardines, discard any bones and chop finely.
  Mash the egg yolks, then mix with the sardines, breadcrumbs, mayonnaise and lemon juice. Season with salt and pepper to taste and beat until thoroughly blended. Pile the mixture into the egg white halves.
  Garnish with parsley and serve with buttered wholemeal bread.
Serves 4

Chicken and Walnut Pâté

185 g (6 oz) liver sausage
1 clove garlic, crushed
3 tablespoons medium sherry
125 g (4 oz) cooked chicken, chopped
⅔ cup walnuts, roughly chopped
pepper
parsley sprigs to garnish

Mash the liver sausage thoroughly with the garlic and sherry until smooth.

Add the chicken, walnuts and pepper to taste. Spoon into individual dishes and garnish with parsley.

Serve with buttered wholemeal toast.

Serves 4

Smoked Mackerel Pâté

150 g (5 oz) butter
1 teaspoon creamed horseradish
250 g (8 oz) frozen smoked mackerel fillet, thawed
juice of 1 lemon
pinch of cayenne pepper
salt and pepper
lemon twists to garnish

Cream the butter with the horseradish until very soft. Remove the skin from the mackerel, flake and add to the butter. Beat to a fairly smooth paste. Add the lemon juice, cayenne and salt and pepper to taste.

Pile the mixture into a small tureen and garnish with lemon twists. Serve with thin slices of buttered toast.

Serves 4

Artichoke Heart and Bacon Salad

2 × 400 g cans artichoke hearts, drained
4 tablespoons French dressing
60 g (2 oz) lean thick bacon rashers

Toss the artichoke hearts in the French dressing and arrange in a serving dish.

Cut the bacon into strips. Place a frying pan over moderate heat, add the bacon and fry in its own fat until crisp.

Sprinkle the bacon over the salad. Serve immediately.

Serves 4

Avocado with Pears and Black Olives

2 avocados
2 tablespoons lemon juice
6 large black olives
1½ tablespoons mayonnaise
1 × 225 g can pear quarters, drained and diced
salt and pepper

Halve the avocados, discard the stones and rub with a little of the lemon juice to prevent discoloration.

Halve the olives and discard the stones. Set aside 4 halves for garnish; chop the remainder.

Mix the mayonnaise and remaining lemon juice together in a bowl. Add the pears, chopped olives, and salt and pepper to taste.

Pile the mixture into the avocado halves. Garnish each portion with an olive half.
Serves 4

Melon and Anchovy Salad

1 medium melon
1 × 45 g can anchovy fillets
juice of 1 lemon
juice of 1 orange
1 teaspoon caster sugar (optional)
watercress sprigs to garnish

Halve the melon and discard the seeds. Scoop the flesh into a serving dish, using a melon baller (or cut into cubes).

Drain the anchovy fillets, reserving 1 tablespoon of the oil. Cut the anchovies into short slivers and add to the melon.

Mix the lemon and orange juice with the reserved anchovy oil and pour over the salad. Add sugar to taste. Chill before serving, garnished with watercress.
Serves 4

Eggs Mimosa

4 hard-boiled eggs
1 × 42 g can lumpfish caviar
6-8 tablespoons mayonnaise
1 small lettuce to garnish

Halve the eggs lengthways, remove the yolks and arrange the whites in a serving dish. Fill the egg white hollows with the caviar.

Rub the yolks through a sieve and spoon over the caviar, reserving 1 tablespoon for garnish.

Spoon the mayonnaise over the eggs, covering them completely.

Garnish with the reserved egg yolk and lettuce. Serve with thin slices of brown bread.

Serves 4

VARIATION: Replace the caviar with 125 g (4 oz) lumpfish cod's roe, ⅔ cup natural low-fat yogurt and the juice of 1 lemon. Mash these ingredients together, adding salt and pepper to taste, and use to fill the egg whites.

Prawn-Stuffed Cucumbers

1 large cucumber, cut into 8 pieces
90 g (3 oz) cream cheese
2 tablespoons lemon juice
125 g (4 oz) prawns
1 × 99 g can pimientos, drained and chopped
8 mint leaves, chopped
salt and pepper
paprika

Hollow out the centre of each cucumber section to form cup shapes and stand upright on a serving dish.

Mix the cream cheese and lemon juice together. Set aside 8 prawns for garnish. Add the remainder to the cheese mixture, with the pimientos and mint. Season with salt, pepper and paprika to taste; mix well.

Pile the filling into the cucumber cups and garnish with the reserved prawns. Serve with thin slices of buttered brown bread.
Serves 4

Asparagus Gratinée

4 slices wholemeal bread, toasted and buttered
1 × 340 g can asparagus spears, drained
½ cup grated Cheddar cheese
pepper

Arrange the toast in a shallow flameproof dish. Divide the asparagus spears equally between the toast slices and sprinkle with the cheese.

Place under a preheated hot grill for about 4 minutes, until the cheese has melted and is lightly browned. Sprinkle with pepper to taste and serve immediately.
Serves 4

MAIN-COURSE DISHES

Pork Chops with Mustard Sauce

30 g (1 oz) butter
1 onion, finely sliced
1 tablespoon flour
salt and pepper
4 pork chops
½ cup medium sherry
¾ cup chicken stock
2 tablespoons light French mustard

Melt the butter in a flameproof casserole, add the onion and fry until soft. Remove with a slotted spoon and set aside.

Season the flour with salt and pepper and use to coat the chops. Add to the casserole and fry briskly until browned on both sides.

Return the onion to the casserole and add the sherry and stock. Cover and simmer for 30 minutes, or until the chops are cooked.

Transfer the chops to a warmed serving dish, using a slotted spoon. Add the mustard to the sauce in the casserole, stir well and check the seasoning. Pour over the chops and serve immediately.

Serves 4

Pork Fillet with Plums

2 tablespoons plain flour
salt and pepper
500 g (1 lb) pork fillet, cut into 4 pieces
60 g (2 oz) butter
1 × 425 g can purple plums, drained and stoned
¼ teaspoon ground cinnamon
⅔ cup red wine
chopped parsley to garnish

Season the flour with salt and pepper and use to coat the pork.

Melt the butter in a frying pan, add the pork and fry until golden brown on both sides. Transfer to a casserole.

Mash the plums to a coarse purée. Stir in the cinnamon and wine and pour over the pork. Cover and cook in a preheated moderate oven, 180°C (350°F), for 30 minutes.

Serve hot, garnished with parsley.
Serves 4

Barbecued Spare Ribs

1 kg (2 lb) pork spare ribs
4 tablespoons tomato ketchup or sauce
2 tablespoons clear honey
3 tablespoons soy sauce
3 tablespoons wine vinegar
2 teaspoons tomato paste
1 teaspoon salt
1½ cups stock
TO GARNISH:
1-2 spring onions, (green part only), finely chopped

Place the spare ribs in a roasting pan. Mix together the ketchup, honey, soy sauce, vinegar, tomato paste, salt and stock and pour over the ribs. If time, marinate for 2 to 3 hours. Cook in a preheated hot oven, 220°C (425°F), for 15 minutes.

Transfer the spare ribs to a roasting rack. Lower the oven temperature to moderately hot 190°C (375°F), and cook the spare ribs for a further 30 minutes until brown and crisp.

Meanwhile, place the roasting pan over a moderate heat and boil the cooking liquor until reduced to a thick sauce.

Arrange the spare ribs on a serving dish and pour over the sauce. Garnish with the spring onion. Serve with plain boiled rice.
Serves 4

Frankfurter and Bean Hot Pot

30 g (1 oz) butter
1 large onion, chopped
2 bacon rashers, derinded and chopped
4 frankfurters, diced
125 g (4 oz) garlic sausage, diced
1 tablespoon capers, chopped
2 × 110 g cans red kidney beans, drained
2/3 cup light stock
salt and pepper
2 tablespoons chopped parsley

Melt the butter in a flameproof casserole, add the onion and bacon and fry gently until soft. Add the frankfurters, garlic sausage, capers and kidney beans. Mix well.

Stir in the stock. Cover and cook in a preheated moderate oven, 180°C (350°F), for 20 minutes.

Check the seasoning and stir in the parsley. Serve immediately, accompanied by crusty French bread.
Serves 4

Tyrolean Veal with Sour Cream

2 tablespoons plain
 flour
salt and pepper
4 veal scnitzels
60 g (2 oz) butter
1 small onion, finely
 chopped
2 tablespoons capers,
 with their vinegar
¾ cup water
4 tablespoons sour
 cream
chopped parsley to
 garnish

Season half the flour with salt and pepper and use to coat the scnitzels.

Melt half the butter in a frying pan, add the veal and fry gently for about 5 minutes on each side until tender and golden. Remove and set aside.

Melt the remaining butter in the pan, add the onion and fry until soft. Add the remaining flour and cook, stirring, for 1 to 2 minutes.

Add the capers in their vinegar and the water and cook until the sauce thickens. Stir in the sour cream. Return the veal to the pan and heat through gently.

Sprinkle with parsley and serve with plain boiled rice.
Serves 4

Veal Stroganoff

4 veal scnitzels
60 g (2 oz) butter
1 onion, sliced
125 g (4 oz) button
  mushrooms, sliced
1-2 tablespoons
  tomato paste
1 tablespoon plain
  flour
½ cup sour cream
salt and pepper
1-2 tablespoons
  lemon juice
watercress sprigs to
  garnish

Beat the scnitzels until thin, then cut into short strips.

Melt half the butter in a frying pan, add the onion and mushrooms and fry until soft. Stir in the tomato paste and flour. Cook, stirring over low heat for 2 to 3 minutes. Remove from the heat.

Melt the remaining butter in a clean pan, add the veal and fry over high heat, turning, until evenly browned. Add the meat to the sauce and stir well. Add the cream, salt, pepper and lemon juice to taste.

Garnish with watercress. Serve immediately, with buttered noodles or plain boiled rice.

Serves 4

Lamb and Apple Pie

250 g (8 oz) cooked lamb, finely chopped
250 g (8 oz) cooked ham, finely chopped
1 large cooking apple, peeled, cored and diced
1 large onion, chopped
salt and pepper
1 teaspoon chopped rosemary
¾ cup chicken stock
¾ cup cider
1 × 250 g packet frozen shortcrust pastry, thawed
beaten egg to glaze

Place the lamb, ham, apple and onion in a 6 cup pie dish, mix well and sprinkle with salt and pepper to taste and the rosemary. Pour over the stock and cider.

Roll out the pastry on a lightly floured board to a round slightly larger than the dish. Cut off a 2.5 cm (1 inch) strip all round, dampen and place along the edge of the dish.

Dampen the pastry strip and put the pastry lid in position. Knock up and flute the edges of the pastry. Cut a slit in the top and decorate with pastry leaves cut from any trimmings.

Brush with beaten egg and bake in a preheated moderately hot oven, 190°C (375°F), for 35 minutes or until the pastry is cooked and golden.
Serves 4

Barbecued Lamb Cutlets

4 drops Tabasco sauce
1-2 teaspoons chilli powder
2 teaspoons salt
1½ tablespoons brown sugar
1½ tablespoons Worcestershire sauce
2 tablespoons tomato ketchup or sauce
1 tablespoon wine vinegar
4 tablespoons water
8 lamb cutlets, trimmed

Mix the Tabasco, chilli powder, salt and brown sugar together in a large dish. Gradually stir in the Worcestershire sauce, tomato ketchup, vinegar and water. Add the cutlets and turn to coat thoroughly. Leave to marinate for 4 hours.

Transfer the cutlets to a grill rack and brush with the marinade. Cook under a preheated hot grill for 5 to 10 minutes on each side, depending on the thickness of the cutlets, basting frequently with the marinade.

Serve immediately with plain boiled rice or buttered noodles.
Serves 4

London Pie

500 g (1 lb) minced beef
2 onions, chopped
⅓ cup sultanas
2 cooking apples, peeled, cored and chopped
2 tablespoons tomato paste
4 tablespoons beef stock
salt and pepper
½ × 125 g packet instant mashed potato
½ cup milk
½ cup water
½ cup grated Cheddar cheese
parsley sprigs to garnish

Mix together the beef, onions, sultanas and apples in a casserole. Blend the tomato purée with the stock and add to the beef mixture. Season with salt and pepper to taste.

Cover with foil and cook in a preheated moderate oven, 180°C (350°F), for 30 minutes.

Make up the potato, using the milk and water, as directed on the packet. Spoon over the top of the pie. Sprinkle with cheese and return to the oven for about 15 minutes, until the cheese is melted and browned.

Garnish with parsley and serve immediately.

Serves 4

Chilli con Carne

60 g (2 oz) butter
2 large onions, finely chopped
2 cloves garlic, crushed
500 g (1 lb) minced beef
1-2 teaspoons chilli powder
4 teaspoons cumin powder
¼ cup tomato paste
2 × 440 g cans red kidney beans, drained
1¼ cups beef stock
salt and pepper
chopped parsley to garnish

Melt the butter in a flameproof casserole. Add the onions and garlic and fry gently for 5 minutes until golden. Stir in the beef and cook, stirring, for 10 minutes.

Mix together the chilli powder, cumin and tomato paste and stir into the beef. Add the kidney beans, stock and salt and pepper to taste.

Cover and cook in a preheated moderate oven, 180°C (350°F), for 25 minutes.

Sprinkle with chopped parsley and serve hot, with plain boiled rice or crusty French bread.

Serves 4

Liver and Bacon with Apple Rings

60 g (2 oz) butter
2 large cooking apples, peeled, cored and cut into thick rings
500 g (1 lb) calves' liver, sliced
4 rashers lean bacon, derinded

Melt half the butter in a frying pan, add the apple rings and fry gently until soft. Transfer to a warmed dish; keep hot.

Melt the remaining butter in the pan, add the liver and fry gently for about 2 minutes on each side until tender.

Meanwhile, cook the bacon under a preheated medium grill until crisp.

Transfer the liver to a warmed serving dish. Arrange the apple rings on top and the bacon around the edge. Serve immediately.
Serves 4

Steak aux Poivres

1-2 tablespoons black
  peppercorns
4 fillet or rump
  steaks
60 g (2 oz) butter
2 tablespoons
  brandy, warmed
¾ cup cream
salt

Crush the peppercorns and press them into both sides of the steaks. Leave to stand for 15 minutes.

Melt the butter in a heavy pan and fry the steaks quickly for 2 minutes on each side. Lower the heat and cook for a further 3 to 7 minutes on each side, until cooked to taste. Transfer to a warmed serving dish and keep hot.

Add the brandy to the juices in the pan and ignite. When the flames have died down, stir in the cream. Cook briskly for 2 minutes, stirring constantly. Add salt to taste. Pour the sauce over the steaks and serve immediately.

Serves 4

NOTE: If available, use green peppercorns instead of black ones for a more subtle flavour.

Roast Beef Salad with Sour Cream and Olives

500 g (1 lb) rare roast beef, thickly sliced
¾ cup sour cream
juice of 1 lemon
125 g (4 oz) black olives, halved and stoned

Cut the beef slices into strips and place in a serving dish. Mix together the sour cream and lemon juice. Add half the olives to the beef slices and spoon over the cream.

Garnish with the remaining olives. Serve with jacket potatoes and side salads of choice.

Serves 4

Cold Tongue Giardinera

125 g (4 oz) frozen mixed vegetables, lightly cooked
2 pickled onions, chopped
2 gherkins, chopped
6 stuffed olives, sliced
60 g (2 oz) capers, chopped
4 tablespoons French dressing
1 tablespoon vinegar (from the pickles)
375 g (12 oz) cooked tongue, thinly sliced
4 hard-boiled eggs, sliced
chopped parsley to garnish

Put the vegetables in a bowl with the pickled onions, gherkins, olives, capers, French dressing and pickling vinegar. Leave to marinate for 4 hours.

Arrange the tongue slices on a serving dish and spoon over the vegetable mixture. Garnish with egg slices and parsley. Serve cold, with crusty bread rolls.
Serves 4

Spiced Country Chicken

4 chicken portions
2 tablespoons plain flour
30 g (1 oz) butter
1 onion, finely chopped
1 clove garlic, crushed
1 green pepper, cored, seeded and chopped
2 teaspoons curry powder
1 teaspoon chopped thyme
½ × 425 g can tomatoes
2 tablespoons sweet white vermouth
salt and pepper
⅓ cup raisins

Coat the chicken portions with flour. Melt the butter in a large pan, add the chicken and fry briskly until golden all over. Remove from the pan and set aside.

Add the onion, garlic, green pepper, curry powder and thyme to the fat remaining in the pan and fry, stirring, for 5 minutes.

Add the tomatoes with their juice and the vermouth. Return the chicken to the pan and add salt and pepper to taste. Cover and cook for 20 minutes, or until the chicken is tender.

Stir in the raisins and serve hot, with jacket potatoes or plain boiled rice.

Serves 4

Chicken with Oranges and Almonds

60 g (2 oz) butter
½ cup flaked almonds
4 chicken portions
salt and pepper
paprika
3 oranges
2 teaspoons caster sugar

Melt the butter in a pan, add the almonds and fry gently until golden. Remove with a slotted spoon and set aside.

Sprinkle the chicken with salt, pepper and paprika to taste. Add to the fat remaining in the pan and fry, turning, until golden all over. Cover and cook gently for 30 minutes, or until tender.

Meanwhile, squeeze the juice from two of the oranges. Carefully cut the third orange into segments, discarding all pith.

Transfer the chicken to a warmed serving dish and keep hot.

Add the orange juice, orange segments and sugar to the pan juices and boil rapidly for 2 minutes. Pour over the chicken. Sprinkle with the almonds and serve immediately.

Serves 4

Pineapple Chicken

4 chicken portions
1 onion, thinly sliced
1 teaspoon salt
¼ teaspoon pepper
½ teaspoon dried rosemary
½ teaspoon ground ginger
pinch of paprika
1 × 425 g can unsweetened pineapple juice
chopped parsley to garnish

Put the chicken in a casserole dish. Sprinkle with the onion, salt, pepper, rosemary, ginger and paprika and pour over the pineapple juice.

Cook in a preheated moderate oven, 180°C (350°F), for 45 minutes or until the chicken is cooked and browned on top. Serve hot, garnished with parsley.

Serves 4

Chicken and Walnut Salad

500 g (1 lb) cooked boned chicken
2 celery sticks, coarsely chopped
1 large dessert apple, cored and diced
½ cup walnuts, roughly chopped
4 tablespoons mayonnaise
1-2 tablespoons cream (optional)
watercress sprigs to garnish

Cut the chicken into pieces and place in a large bowl with the celery, apple and walnuts.

Thin the mayonnaise if necessary to give the consistency of thick cream, by adding a little cream. Pour over the chicken and toss well until the ingredients are evenly coated.

Turn into a serving dish and garnish with watercress.

Serves 4

Seafood Curry

2 tablespoons oil
2 onions, chopped
½ red pepper, cored, seeded and chopped
2 celery sticks, chopped
60 g (2 oz) mushrooms, sliced
1 tablespoon curry powder
½ teaspoon turmeric
½ teaspoon ground ginger
1 cooking apple, peeled, cored and diced
250 g (8 oz) fish fillet diced
125 g (4 oz) prawns
⅓ cup raisins
1 teaspoon Worcestershire sauce
2 teaspoons tomato paste
4 tablespoons white wine
6 tablespoons water
salt and pepper
2 tablespoons natural low-fat yogurt
juice of ½ lemon

Heat the oil in a large pan. Add the onions, pepper, celery and mushrooms and fry gently for 5 minutes. Add the curry powder, turmeric and ginger and cook, stirring, for 2 minutes.

Add the apple, fish fillets, prawns, raisins, Worcestershire sauce and tomato paste and stir well. Stir in the wine and water and season with salt and pepper to taste. Cover and simmer gently for 10 minutes.

Just before serving, stir in the yogurt and lemon juice. Serve with plain boiled rice.

Serves 4

Fish and Egg Mornay

4 smoked fish fillets, skinned
2 cups milk
1 bouquet garni
4 eggs
45 g (1½ oz) butter
¼ cup plain flour
¾ cup grated Cheddar cheese
pepper
parsley sprigs to garnish

Place the fish fillets in a pan with the milk and bouquet garni. Cook over low heat for 10 minutes or until tender. Transfer to a warmed serving dish, using a slotted spoon, and keep hot. Strain the milk and reserve.

Poach the eggs in simmering water for 4 to 5 minutes. Meanwhile, melt the butter in a pan. Stir in the flour and cook, stirring, for 2 minutes. Blend in the milk and simmer, stirring, until thickened. Stir in two-thirds of the cheese.

Using a slotted spoon, place a poached egg on each fish fillet. Top with the cheese sauce and sprinkle with the remaining cheese and pepper to taste. Place under a preheated hot grill until lightly browned. Serve immediately, garnished with parsley.

Serves 4

Fish and Potato Pie

375 g (12 oz) bream or gemfish fillet
1 × 220 g can button mushrooms, drained
1 × 425 g can tomatoes
125 g (4 oz) peeled prawns
1 × 300 ml packet onion sauce mix
¾ cup milk
⅔ cup white wine
½ × 125 g packet instant mashed potato
4-6 tablespoons water
salt and pepper
30 g (1 oz) butter
TO GARNISH:
tomato slices
parsley sprigs

Cut the fish fillets into large pieces and place in a casserole. Cover with the mushrooms and tomatoes and pour over a little of the tomato juice. Sprinkle the prawns on top.

Make up the onion sauce as directed on the packet, using ⅔ cup of the milk and the wine. Pour over the prawns.

Make up the potato as directed on the packet, using the remaining milk and the water. Add salt and pepper to taste. Spoon over the fish mixture to cover completely. Dot with the butter.

Bake in a preheated moderate oven, 180°C (350°F), for 30 minutes, until the top is golden brown. Serve hot, garnished with tomato and parsley.

Serves 4

Baked Trout

60 g (2 oz) butter
4 trout, cleaned
1 lemon, sliced
5 tablespoons dry white wine
1 teaspoon dried tarragon
salt and pepper
parsley sprigs to garnish

Line a baking dish with a large piece of foil, allowing sufficient to hang over the sides. Spread the butter over the foil. Lay the trout in the dish and arrange the lemon slices on top.

Mix together the wine, tarragon and salt and pepper to taste and pour over the fish.

Fold the foil over the trout to make a parcel and fold the edges together to seal. Cook in a preheated moderate oven, 180°C (350°F), for 30 minutes.

Transfer the trout to a warmed serving dish. Pour over the juices and garnish with parsley.

Serves 4

Pacific Tuna Pie

- 2 × 200 g cans tuna fish, drained and flaked
- 1 × 310 g can sweetcorn, drained
- 1 × 113 g packet frozen peas
- 1 × 305 g can condensed chicken soup
- 1 × 425 g can tomatoes, drained
- ¾ cup grated Cheddar cheese
- 1 × 75 g packet potato crisps, crushed

Mix together the tuna, sweetcorn, peas and soup. Turn into a buttered casserole and cover with the tomatoes.

Mix together the cheese and crisps and sprinkle over the tomatoes. Cook in a preheated moderately hot oven, 190°C (375°F), for 30 minutes, until the top is golden and bubbling.

Serve hot, with baked tomatoes if liked.

Serves 4

Fish in Caper Mayonnaise

4 fish fillets, skinned
salt and pepper
⅔ cup dry white wine
½ lemon, sliced
6 tablespoons mayonnaise
4 tablespoons lemon juice
60 g (2 oz) capers, chopped

Place the fish in a frying pan and sprinkle with salt and pepper to taste. Add the wine and lemon slices, cover and simmer for 15-20 minutes.

Remove the fish from the pan, reserving 2 tablespoons of the cooking liquor, and leave to cool.

Mix together the mayonnaise, lemon juice and the reserved liquor. Stir in the capers.

Place the fish in a serving dish and top with the caper sauce. Serve cold.
Serves 4

Prawn and Artichoke Vol-au-Vents

1 × 300 ml packet onion sauce mix
⅔ cup milk
⅔ cup dry white wine
125 g (4 oz) frozen peas
1 × 400 g can artichoke hearts, drained and quartered
375 g (12 oz) frozen peeled prawns, thawed
2 tablespoons cream
celery salt
white pepper
8 frozen vol-au-vent cases
parlsey sprigs to garnish

Make up the sauce mix, following the direction on the packet, using the milk and wine. Add the peas, artichoke hearts and prawns. Simmer gently for 4 minutes.

Add the cream and season with celery salt and pepper to taste.

Cook the vol-au-vent cases from frozen, according to packet directions. Spoon in the prawn mixture and garnish with parsley. Serve immediately.
Serves 4

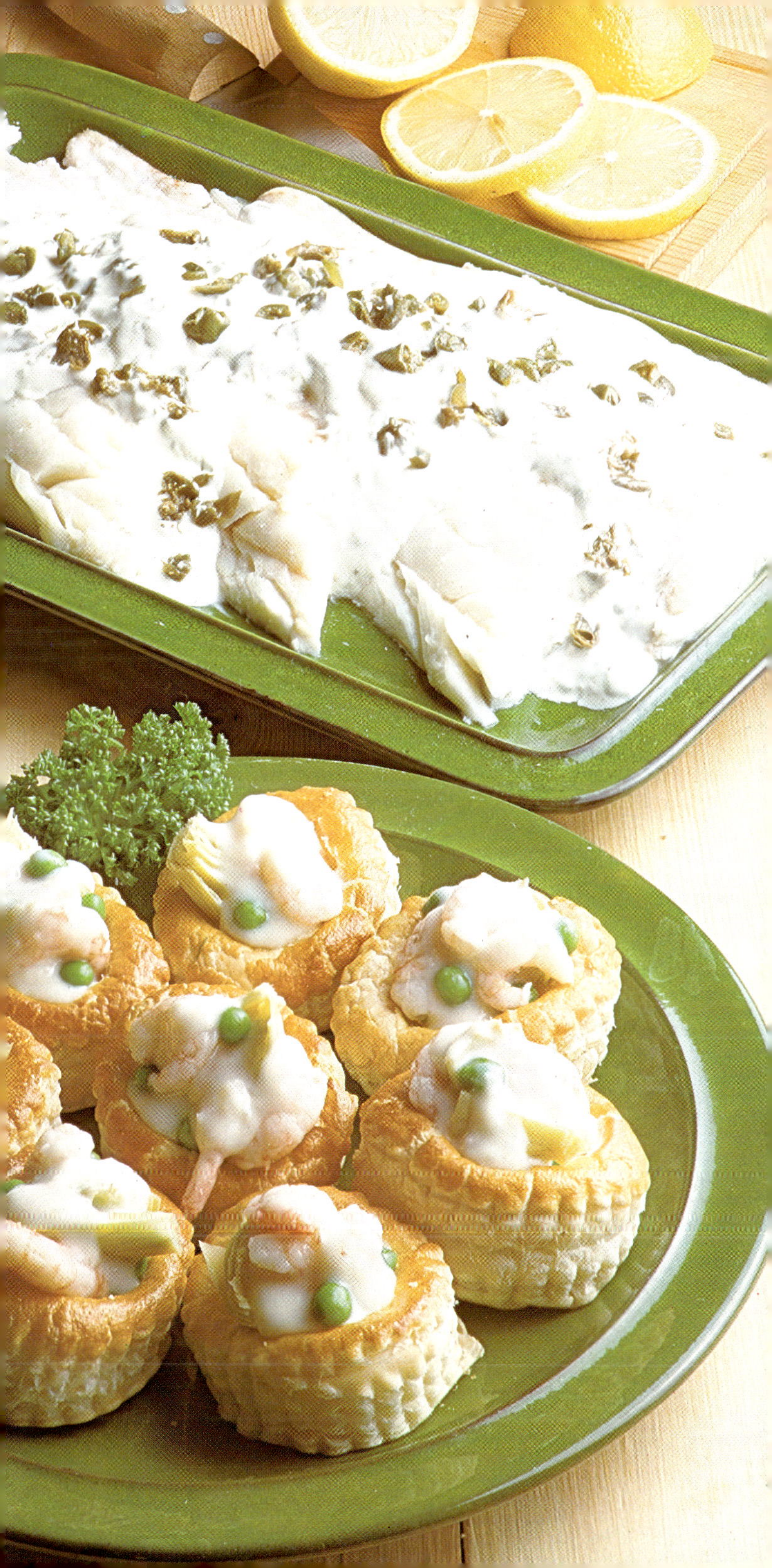

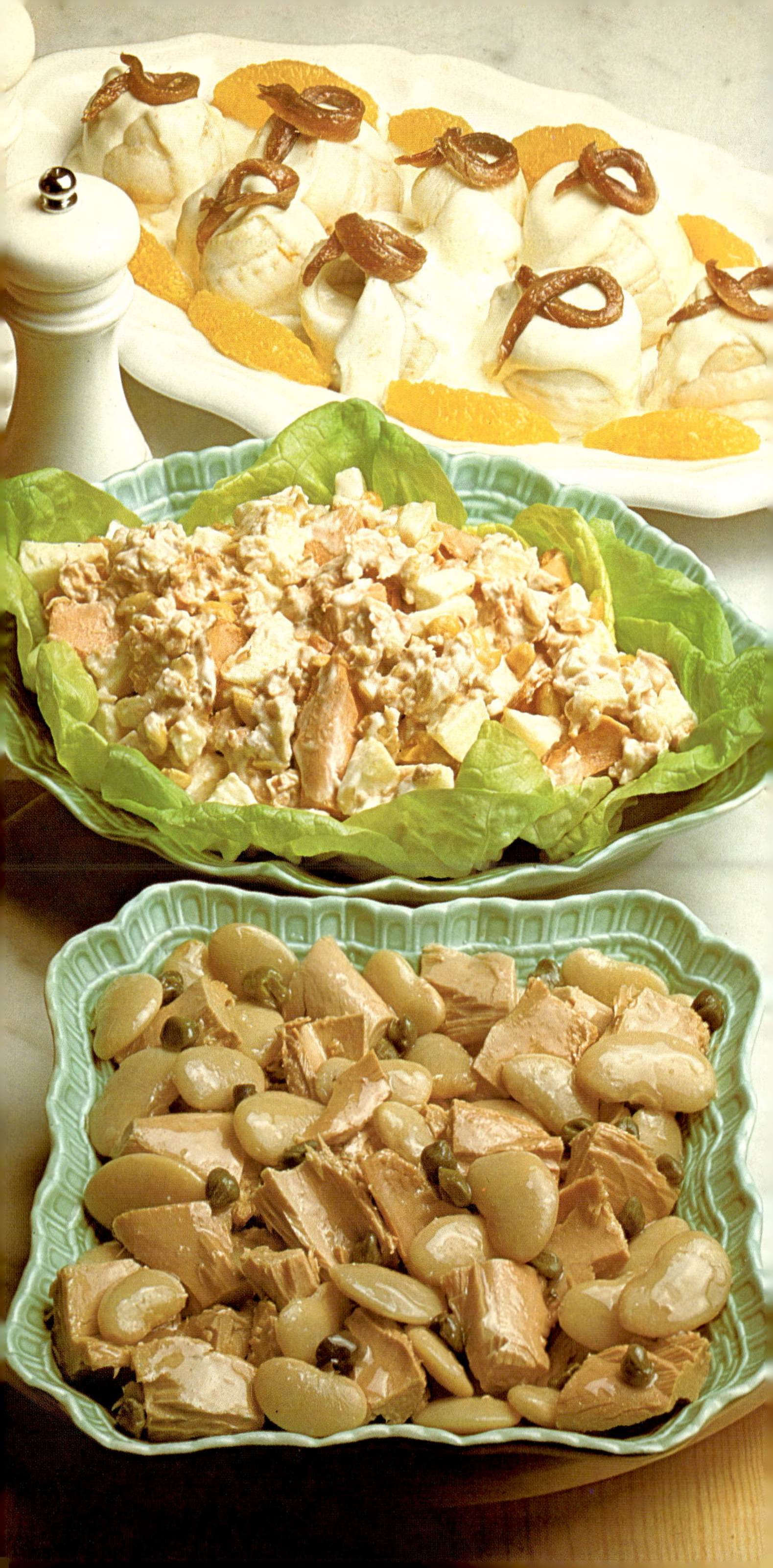

Fish in Orange Mayonnaise

8 thin fish fillets, skinned
grated rind and juice of 2 oranges
juice of 1 lemon
salt and pepper
2/3 cup mayonnaise
TO GARNISH:
anchovy fillets
orange segments

Sprinkle the fish with the rind and juice of 1 orange, the lemon juice, and salt and pepper to taste. Roll up and place in a buttered ovenproof dish. Cover and cook in a preheated moderate oven, 180°C (350°F), for 20 minutes or until just tender. Leave to cool.

Add the remaining grated orange rind and juice to the mayonnaise and mix well.

Place the fish in a serving dish and pour over the mayonnaise. Garnish with anchovy fillets and orange segments. Serve cold.
Serves 4

Crunchy Salmon Salad

3 tablespoons mayonnaise
4 tablespoons lemon juice
2 × 220 g cans red salmon
2 dessert apples, peeled, cored and diced
185 g (6 oz) salted peanuts, chopped
salt and pepper
1 lettuce

Mix the mayonnaise and lemon juice together in a bowl. Drain the salmon, flake and add to the mayonnaise. Stir in the apples, peanuts and salt and pepper to taste.

Line a serving dish with lettuce leaves and pile the salmon mixture into the centre.
Serves 4-6

Tuna and Bean Salad

1 × 100 g and 1 × 200 g can tuna fish, drained and flaked
1 × 440 g can butter beans, drained
4 tablespoons French dressing
chopped capers to garnish

Mix the tuna and butter beans together. Pour over the French dressing and toss well to coat.

Turn into a serving dish and garnish with capers.
Serves 4

VEGETABLES & SALADS

Spinach with Onion and Bacon

2 tablespoons oil
4 bacon rashers, derinded and chopped
1 onion, chopped
1-2 garlic cloves, crushed
500 g (1 lb) spinach leaves
1 tablespoon lemon juice
salt and pepper

Heat the oil in a large pan. Add the bacon, onion and garlic and fry gently for 5 minutes.

Add the spinach, lemon juice and salt and pepper to taste. Fry gently for 3 to 5 minutes, stirring constantly, until the spinach is just tender. Serve immediately.

Serves 4

Celery with Walnuts

1 × 524 g can celery hearts
30 g (1 oz) butter
⅓ cup walnut pieces

Place the celery hearts, with their juice, in a saucepan over moderate heat. When hot, drain, place in a warmed serving dish and keep hot.

Melt the butter in a small pan, add the walnuts and fry until just beginning to brown. Spoon over the celery and serve immediately.
Serves 4

Mushroom and Onion Casserole

60 g (2 oz) butter
500 g (1 lb) onions, roughly chopped
500 g (1 lb) mushrooms, sliced
¾ cup stock
2 tablespoons sherry
2 tablespoons lemon juice
salt and pepper
chopped parsley to garnish

Melt the butter in a flameproof casserole. Add the onions and fry gently for 10 minutes, until soft. Add the mushrooms, stock, sherry, lemon juice, and salt and pepper to taste.

Cover and cook in a preheated moderate oven, 180°C (350°F), for 15 minutes. Serve hot, garnished with parsley.
Serves 4-6

Herb-Glazed Carrots

1 × 850 g can baby carrots
30 g (1 oz) butter
2 teaspoons sugar
6 mint leaves, finely chopped

Heat the carrots with their juice in a saucepan over moderate heat; drain.

Place the butter and sugar in a small pan. Heat gently,stirring, until dissolved, then add the mint. Add the carrots and toss well. Turn into a warmed serving dish. Serve hot.
Serves 4
NOTE: Frozen small whole carrots may be used instead of canned ones: Plunge 500 g (1 lb) frozen carrots into boiling salted water and cook for 5 to 10 minutes until tender.

Baked Onions

4 large or 8 medium onions, unpeeled
salt and pepper
chopped parsley to garnish

Cut a small piece off the root end of each onion. Cut off the tops and make 4 vertical slits through the skin from the top to the middle of each onion.

Place on a baking sheet and cook in a preheated moderate oven, 180°C (350°F), for 30 to 45 minutes, depending on the size of the onions, until the centres are tender.

Remove the skins from the onions. Season with salt and pepper to taste and garnish with parsley. Serve Hot.
Serves 4

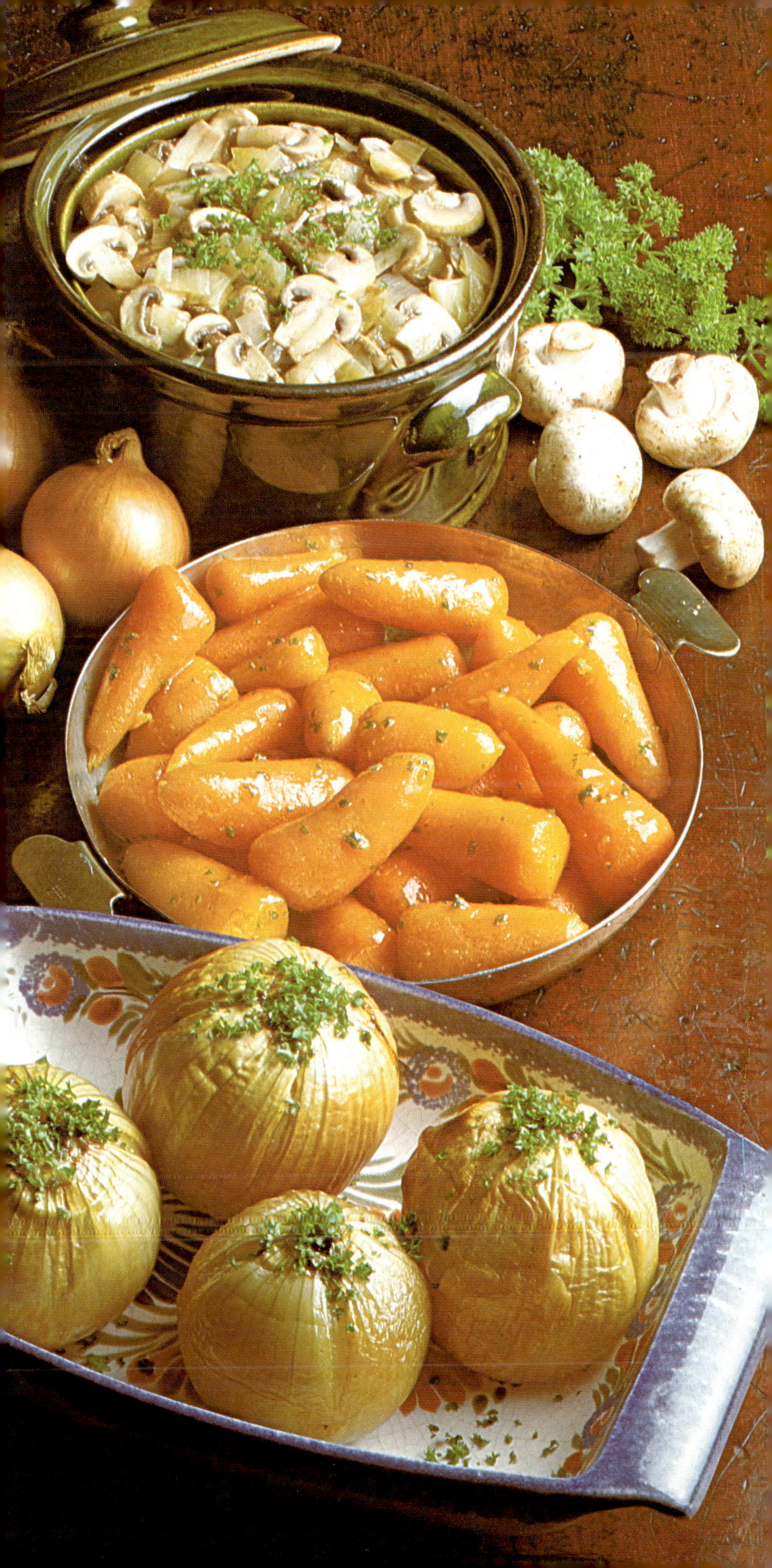

Corn Fritters

1 × 310 g can sweetcorn, drained
2 teaspoons brown sugar
3 eggs, beaten
60 g (2 oz) butter, melted
4 tablespoons grated Parmesan cheese
salt and pepper
oil for deep-frying
watercress sprigs to garnish

Put the sweetcorn in a bowl. Add the sugar, eggs, butter, cheese and salt and pepper to taste. Mix thoroughly.

Heat the oil in a deep-fryer to 180°C (350°F). Drop tablespoonfuls of the corn mixture into the hot oil and fry for about 4 minutes, until crisp and golden.

Remove with a slotted spoon, drain on kitchen paper and serve warm, garnished with watercress.
Serves 4

Crispy Corn Bake

¼ cup plain flour
2 eggs, beaten
2 tablespoons brown sugar
30 g (1 oz) butter, melted
4 tablespoons milk
salt and pepper
2 × 310 g cans sweetcorn, drained
1 × 75 g packet potato crisps, crushed
parsley sprigs to garnish

Put the flour in a bowl and gradually add the eggs, sugar, butter and milk, beating constantly to give a smooth mixture. Season with salt and pepper to taste and stir in the sweetcorn.

Spoon the mixture into an ovenproof dish and sprinkle the crisps over the top.

Bake in a preheated moderately hot oven, 190°C (375°F), for 35 minutes until golden and firm. Serve hot, garnished with parsley.
Serves 4

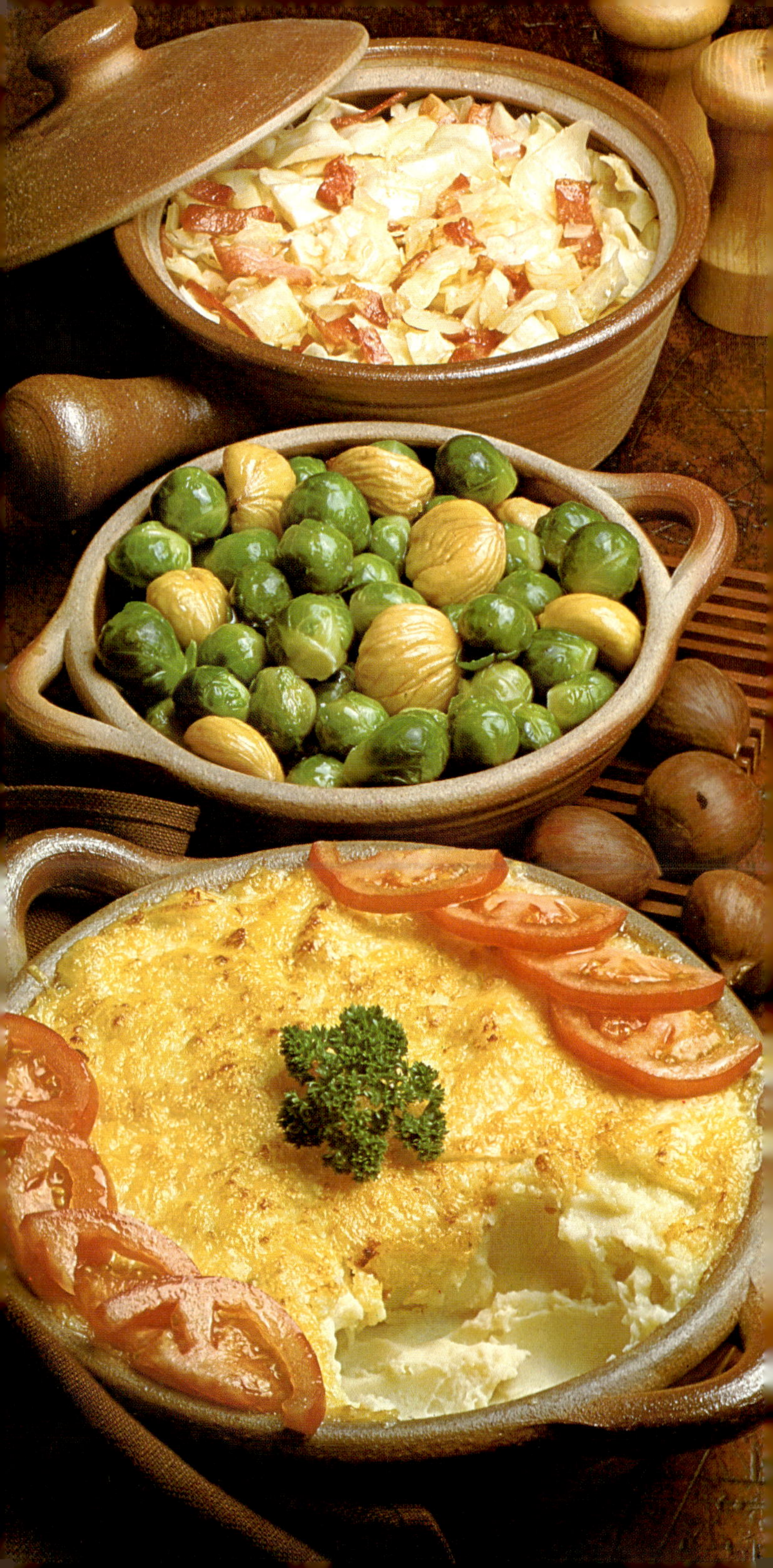

Braised Cabbage with Bacon

2 rashers bacon, derinded and chopped
1 small white cabbage, roughly chopped
1 onion, chopped
6 tablespoons natural low-fat yogurt
6 tablespoons chicken stock
1 teaspoon paprika
salt and pepper

Place a frying pan over moderate heat, add the bacon and cook briskly until crisp. Transfer to an ovenproof dish and add the cabbage and onion.

Mix the yogurt and stock together with the paprika and salt and pepper to taste. Pour over the cabbage.

Cover and cook in a preheated moderate oven, 180°C (350°F), for 40 minutes, stirring halfway through cooking.
Serves 4

Brussels Sprouts with Chestnuts

125 g (4 oz) chestnuts
1 × 375 g pack frozen Brussels sprouts
salt
30 g (1 oz) butter

Score the chestnuts around the middle and place on a baking tray. Bake in a preheated moderate oven, 180°C (350°F), for 10 minutes. When cool enough to handle, peel the chestnuts.

Cook the sprouts in boiling salted water for 3 to 5 minutes.

Meanwhile, melt the butter in a shallow pan. Add the chestnuts and fry briskly, turning, for 2 minutes.

Drain the sprouts and place in a serving dish. Add the chestnuts and butter. Serve immediately.
Serves 4

Potato and Cheese Pie

750 g (1½ lb) boiled potatoes, mashed
salt and pepper
grated nutmeg
60 g (2 oz) butter
¾ cup grated Cheddar cheese
TO GARNISH:
tomato slices
parsley sprigs

Season the potato with salt, pepper and nutmeg to taste and beat in half the butter. Spread the mixture in a shallow ovenproof dish. Top with the cheese and remaining butter.

Cook in a preheated moderate oven, 180°C (350°F), for 15 minutes, then place under a preheated hot grill for 3 minutes.

Sprinkle with pepper and garnish with tomato and parsley. Serve hot.
Serves 4

Carrot and Raisin Salad

500 g (1 lb) carrots, grated
½ cup raisins
2 tablespoons soy sauce
chopped parsley to garnish

Put the carrot and raisins in a serving dish and mix well.

Sprinkle over the soy sauce and toss well. Garnish with chopped parsley.

Serves 4

NOTE: As a variation, replace half the carrots with coarsely grated white cabbage.

Tomatoes with Horseradish Mayonnaise

4 large tomatoes, sliced
3 tablespoons mayonnaise
1 tablespoon creamed horseradish
1-2 tablespoons cream (optional)
chopped parsley to garnish

Arrange the tomatoes in a serving dish. Mix the mayonnaise with the horseradish, adding a little cream if necessary to give the consistency of thick cream.

Spoon the dressing over the tomatoes and sprinkle with parsley.
Serves 4

Green and White Vegetable Salad

60 g (2 oz) frozen green peas, thawed
125 g (4 oz) white cabbage, thinly sliced
2 celery sticks, chopped
1 small green pepper, cored, seeded and chopped
½ onion or ½ leek, thinly sliced
125 g (4 oz) Brussels sprouts, quartered
125 g (4 oz) bean sprouts
4 tablespoons French dressing

Mix all the vegetables together in a salad bowl. Pour over the dressing and toss well. Serve immediately.
Serves 4

Cabbage Salad with Peanut Dressing

- ½ small white cabbage, finely sliced
- 125 g (4 oz) salted peanuts, chopped
- 2 red peppers, cored, seeded and finely chopped
- 1 teaspoon anchovy essence (optional)
- 1 tablespoon soy sauce
- 2 tablespoons lemon juice
- 1 teaspoon cayenne pepper
- ½ teaspoon salt
- 1 teaspoon brown sugar

Put the cabbage in a salad bowl. Combine the remaining ingredients to form a crunchy sauce. Spoon over the cabbage and serve immediately.
Serves 4

Beetroot and Orange Salad

2 large oranges
4 tablespoons French dressing
1 clove garlic, finely sliced (optional)
500 g (1 lb) cooked beetroot, sliced
watercress or mint sprigs to garnish

Grate the rind from one of the oranges and mix with the dressing. Add the garlic, if using. Peel and thinly slice both oranges, removing all pith.

Arrange the orange and beetroot slices in alternate layers in a serving dish. Pour the dressing over the top and garnish with watercress or mint sprigs. Chill before using.

Serves 4

Date and Nut Salad

185 g (6 oz) dates, stoned and halved
3 crisp dessert apples, cored and sliced
½ cup walnut pieces
3 tablespoons lemon juice
⅔ cup natural low-fat yogurt
salt

Put the dates, apples and walnuts in a serving bowl.

Mix together the lemon juice and yogurt. Add salt to taste. Pour over the salad and toss well until the ingredients are evenly coated.
Serves 4

SNACKS & SUPPER DISHES

Egg Florentine

750 g (1½ lb) frozen leaf spinach, thawed and well drained
60 g (2 oz) butter
grated nutmeg
salt and pepper
4 eggs
4 tablespoons grated Parmesan cheese

Place the spinach and half the butter in a large pan. Add nutmeg, salt and pepper to taste. Cook gently for 2 to 3 minutes until tender. Transfer to a shallow ovenproof dish.

Make 4 hollows in the spinach and carefully break an egg into each one. Sprinkle 1 tablespoon cheese over each egg and dot with the remaining butter.

Cook in a preheated moderate oven, 180°C (350°F), for 15 minutes or until the eggs are cooked.

Sprinkle with pepper. Serve immediately, accompanied by wholemeal bread.

Serves 4

Curried Egg Salad

2/3 cup mayonnaise
3 tablespoons cream
1/2-1 tablespoon curry paste
salt and pepper
6 hard-boiled eggs, quartered
1 crisp lettuce
salad cress or watercress to garnish

Mix together the mayonnaise, cream and curry paste. Season with salt and pepper to taste. Carefully fold in the eggs.

Line a serving dish with the lettuce. Pile the egg mixture in the centre and garnish with cress or watercress.

Serves 4

English Rarebit

60 g (2 oz) butter
375 ml can beer
375 g (12 oz) mature Cheddar cheese
1 tablespoon cornflour
1 tablespoon Meaux mustard
1 teaspoon anchovy essence (optional)
1 teaspoon Worcestershire sauce
salt and pepper
4 slices wholemeal bread, toasted and buttered
parsley sprigs to garnish

Melt the butter in a pan, add half the can of beer and the cheese. Heat gently until the cheese is melted.

Blend the cornflour with the remaining beer and add to the pan. Cook gently until the mixture thickens, then add the mustard, anchovy essence, Worcestershire sauce and salt to taste.

Arrange the toast slices in a shallow flameproof dish and pour over the cheese mixture. Place under a preheated hot grill for 3 to 4 minutes until golden and bubbling.

Sprinkle with pepper to taste and garnish with parsley. Serve immediately.
Serves 4

Creamy Herbed Noodles

500 g (1 lb) noodles
salt and pepper
60 g (2 oz) butter
1 small onion, finely chopped
1 clove garlic, crushed
1 cup cream
1 cup dry white wine
2 tomatoes, skinned, seeded and chopped
1 teaspoon green peppercorns (optional)
2 tablespoons chopped chives
4 mint leaves, chopped
4 tablespoons grated Parmesan cheese

Cook the noodles in plenty of boiling salted water for 9 minutes or until *al dente* (cooked but still firm to the bite).

Meanwhile, melt the butter in a small pan, add the onion and garlic and fry gently until soft and translucent. Add the cream, wine, tomatoes and peppercorns, if using, and heat to just below boiling point. Simmer gently for 4 minutes.

Drain the noodles and place in a warmed serving dish. Add the chives and mint to the sauce. Check the seasoning, adding pepper if green peppercorns have not been used. Pour over the noodles. Sprinkle with the Parmesan cheese.
Serves 4

Egg and Onion Casserole

30 g (1 oz) butter
1¼ cups milk
2 small onions, finely chopped
1 × 300 ml packet onion sauce mix
4 hard-boiled eggs, roughly chopped
4 tablespoons fresh white breadcrumbs

Melt the butter in a pan, add the milk and onions and bring slowly to the boil. Lower the heat, cover and simmer for 4 minutes.

Cool slightly, then gradually stir into the onion sauce mix. Return to the heat and cook until thickened.

Stir in the egg, pour into a small casserole dish and cover with the breadcrumbs.

Place under a preheated hot grill for 3 minutes or until the crumbs are crisp and golden.
Serves 4

French Toasts with Bacon

8 rashers lean bacon, derinded
3 eggs
4 tablespoons milk
salt and pepper
4 thick slices brown or white bread
30 g (1 oz) lard or butter

Place a frying pan over low heat, add the bacon and fry gently in its own fat until quite crisp. Remove from the pan with a slotted spoon and keep warm.

Beat the eggs and milk together, with salt and pepper to taste. Place the bread in a shallow dish and pour over the egg mixture. Leave to soak for a few minutes.

Melt the lard or butter in the frying pan. Transfer the bread slices to the hot fat, using a fish slice, and fry both sides until golden brown. Transfer to serving plates and arrange the bacon slices on top. Serve immediately.
Serves 4

Salmon Savoury

2 × 220 g cans salmon, drained and mashed
2 cups grated Cheddar cheese
3 tablespoons natural low-fat yogurt
3 tablespoons lemon juice
salt and pepper
paprika
4 eggs, beaten
4 slices wholemeal bread, toasted and buttered
lemon wedges to serve

Mix the salmon with the cheese. Stir in the yogurt and lemon juice. Season with salt, pepper and paprika to taste. Beat until well mixed, then beat in the eggs.

Put the toast in a shallow flameproof dish and pile the salmon mixture on top. Place under a preheated low grill for 10 minutes or until the mixture is heated through, then increase the heat and grill for a further 5 minutes to brown the top. Serve immediately, with lemon wedges.
Serves 4

Smoked Fish Soufflé Omelet

60 g (2 oz) butter
2 smoked fish fillets, cooked and flaked
4 tablespoons cream
4 tablespoons grated Parmesan cheese
salt and pepper
6 eggs, separated
parsley sprigs to garnish

Melt half the butter in a saucepan. Add the fish, cream and half the cheese and heat gently until the cheese is melted.

Remove from the heat and season with salt and pepper to taste. Stir in the egg yolks. Whisk the egg whites until stiff and fold into the fish mixture.

Melt the remaining butter in a large frying pan. When sizzling, pour in the omelet mixture. Cook gently for 2 to 3 minutes until set, drawing the cooked edges towards the centre with a fork.

Cut into quarters and turn out on to warmed serving plates. Sprinkle with the remaining cheese and garnish with parsley. Serve immediately.
Serves 4

Spanish Omelet

1 tablespoon oil
1 clove garlic, crushed
2 onions, sliced
125 g (4 oz) canned sweetcorn
1 × 99 g can pimientos, drained and sliced
1 medium potato, boiled and diced
60 g (2 oz) frozen peas
60 g (2 oz) chorizo or garlic sausage, chopped
8 eggs
salt and pepper
2 tablespoons water
30 g (1 oz) butter
watercress sprigs to garnish

Heat the oil in a frying pan, add the garlic and onions and cook for 10 minutes until soft.

Mix the sweetcorn, pimientos, potato, peas and sausage together. Add the onion and garlic.

Beat the eggs together with salt and pepper to taste and the water. Stir in the vegetable mixture.

Melt the butter in a large frying pan. When sizzling, pour in the omelet mixture and cook briskly for 5 minutes or until set, drawing the cooked edges towards the centre during the first minute.

Cut into quarters and turn out onto warmed serving plates. Garnish with watercress and serve immediately.
Serves 4

Savoury Macaroni Cheese

500 g (1 lb)
  macaroni
salt
4 rashers bacon,
  derinded and
  chopped
2 onions, chopped
2 × 300 ml packets
  cheese sauce mix
2½ cups milk
½ cup cream
1½ cups grated
  Cheddar cheese
1 × 425 g can
  tomatoes, drained
  and chopped
TO GARNISH:
tomato slices
parsley sprigs

Cook the macaroni in plenty of boiling salted water for 12 minutes or until *al dente* (cooked but still firm to the bite).

Cook the bacon in a frying pan over low heat until the fat runs. Add the onions and fry gently for 5 minutes.

Make up the cheese sauce with the milk as directed on the packet, then add to the bacon and onions. Stir in the cream and half the cheese. Cook gently until the cheese is melted.

Drain the macaroni and add to the sauce, with the tomatoes; mix well.

Turn into a shallow flameproof dish and top with the remaining cheese. Place under a preheated hot grill for 10 minutes or until the top is crisp and brown. Garnish with tomato and parsley. Serve immediately.

Serves 4-6

Beef and Onion Patties

- 3 tablespoons instant mashed potato
- 4 tablespoons milk
- 4 tablespoons water
- 1 × 340 g can corned beef
- 1 onion, finely chopped
- 1 cup fresh white breadcrumbs
- 2 teaspoons Worcestershire sauce
- 2 teaspoons French mustard
- 2 eggs, beaten
- salt and pepper
- 2 tablespoons vegetable oil

Make up the potato as directed on the packet, using the milk and water.

Mash the corned beef with a fork. Add the onion, potato, breadcrumbs, Worcestershire sauce, mustard and eggs. Beat until thoroughly mixed. Season with salt and pepper to taste.

Heat the oil in a frying pan and add tablespoonfuls of the mixture. Fry gently for about 5 minutes on each side, until firm and golden. Remove and drain on kitchen paper.

Serve hot, accompanied by a crisp green salad.

Serves 4-6

Ham and Mushroom Toasts

1 × 300 ml packet onion sauce mix
1¼ cups milk
375 g (12 oz) button mushrooms, sliced
125 g (4 oz) cooked ham, diced
½ cup natural low-fat yogurt
4 slices brown or white bread, toasted and buttered
pepper
parsley sprigs to garnish

Put the sauce mix in a pan, stir in the milk and heat gently until thickened.

Add the mushrooms and ham. Cover and simmer for 5 minutes or until the mushrooms are tender.

Remove from the heat and stir in the yogurt. Spoon over the toast slices and sprinkle with pepper to taste. Garnish with parsley and serve immediately.

Serves 4

NOTE: This recipe is equally delicious prepared with tongue instead of ham.

Savoury Onion Puffs

30 g (1 oz) butter
375 g (12 oz) onions, chopped
185 g (6 oz) potatoes, boiled and diced
1 × 300 ml packet onion sauce mix
¾ cup milk
125 g (4 oz) grated Cheddar cheese
salt and pepper
1 × 225 g packet frozen puff pastry, thawed
beaten egg to glaze

Melt the butter in a pan, add the onions and cook gently for 5 minutes. Add the potatoes.

Make up the sauce mix with the milk, as directed on the packet. Stir into the onion mixture with the cheese and salt and pepper to taste. Cook for 3 minutes.

Roll out the pastry on a lightly floured board to a 30 cm (12 inch) square and cut into 4 squares. Place on a baking sheet.

Divide the onion mixture between the squares, placing it in the centre of each. Dampen the edges and fold the pastry over the filling to form triangular puffs. Press the edges together to seal, trim, knock up and flute. Brush the pastry with beaten egg.

Cook in a preheated hot oven, 220°C (425°F), for 15 minutes until well risen and golden.
Serves 4

Tomato Fondue

60 g (2 oz) butter
1 small onion, finely chopped
2 cloves garlic, crushed
1 × 820 g can tomatoes
1 teaspoon dried oregano
1 teaspoon paprika
2 teaspoons dried basil
1¼ cups dry white wine
salt and pepper
500 g (1 lb) grated Cheddar cheese
bread cubes to serve

Melt the butter in a fondue dish or flameproof casserole. Add the onion and garlic and fry until softened.

Drain the tomatoes thoroughly, then mash to a pulp. Add to the onion, with the oregano, paprika, basil and wine. Season with salt and pepper to taste. Cook gently for 10 minutes.

Gradually stir in the cheese and cook over a low heat until melted. Check the seasoning. Serve immediately with the bread cubes. Dip these into the hot fondue before eating.
Serves 4-6

Fried Apple and Cheese Sandwiches

2 dessert apples, peeled, cored and grated
1 cup grated Cheddar cheese
1 × 125 g packet cream cheese
2 drops of Tabasco sauce
salt and pepper
8 slices wholemeal bread, buttered
60 g (2 oz) butter

Place the apple, Cheddar, cream cheese and Tabasco in a bowl. Mix until thoroughly blended. Season with salt and pepper to taste.

Divide the mixture between four of the bread slices and spread evenly. Cover with the remaining bread.

Melt half the butter in a frying pan. Add two of the sandwiches and fry gently on both sides until golden and the cheese has melted slightly. Repeat with the remaining butter and sandwiches. Serve immediately.
Serves 4

Baked Cheese and Mustard Pudding

4 thick slices brown or white bread, crusts removed
60 g (2 oz) butter
1 tablespoon English mustard
1½ cups grated Cheddar cheese
pepper
2 eggs
2 egg yolks
⅔ cup chicken stock, cooled
tomato slices to garnish

Spread both sides of the bread thickly with the butter and mustard to taste.

Put 2 slices in a well buttered pie dish. Cover with half the cheese and sprinkle with a little pepper. Top with the remaining bread.

Beat together the eggs and egg yolks and stir in the stock. Pour over the bread and top with the remaining cheese.

Cook in a preheated moderately hot oven, 190°C (375°F), for 25 to 30 minutes until golden.

Garnish with tomato slices and serve immediately.

Serves 4

Baked Eggs in Orange Potatoes

½ × 125 g packet instant mashed potato
½ cup milk
½ cup water
salt and pepper
½ small onion, finely chopped
grated rind of 1 orange
2 egg yolks
2 slices cooked ham, finely chopped
4 eggs
½ cup grated Cheddar cheese
30 g (1 oz) butter
watercress sprigs to garnish

Make up the potato as directed on the packet, using the milk and water. Season liberally with salt and pepper and beat in the onion, orange rind and egg yolks.

Spread in a shallow ovenproof dish and make 4 hollows in the potato. Line each hollow with chopped ham and carefully break an egg into each one. Sprinkle the eggs with cheese and dot with butter.

Sprinkle with pepper to taste and bake in a preheated moderately hot oven, 190°C (375°F), for 20 minutes, or until the eggs are firm.

Garnish with watercress and serve immediately.

Serves 4

DESSERTS

Yogurt Cheesecake

185 g (6 oz) cream cheese
2/3 cup natural low-fat yogurt
2 drops vanilla essence
2 tablespoons thick honey
2 teaspoons lemon juice
1 × 15-18 cm (6-7 inch) sponge flan case
125 g (4 oz) frozen blackberries or boysenberries, thawed

Beat the cheese and yogurt together until smooth. Add the vanilla essence, honey and lemon juice and beat until thoroughly blended.

Spoon into the flan case and top with the blackberries or boysenberries. Chill before serving.
Serves 4

Moroccan Orange Salad

4 large or 6 medium oranges
1/3 cup dates, roughly chopped
1/4 cup flaked almonds
2 tablespoons caster sugar
juice of 2 lemons
ground cinnamon to decorate

Peel and slice the oranges, discarding the pith. Place in a serving dish with the dates and almonds.

Mix together the sugar and lemon juice and pour over the fruit mixture. Chill for at least 2 hours before serving.

Sprinkle with cinnamon to taste. Serve with cream, if liked.

Serves 4

Treacle Tart

1 × 225 g packet frozen shortcrust pastry, thawed
4 tablespoons cornflakes, crushed, or fresh white breadcrumbs
5 tablespoons golden syrup, warmed
juice of ½ lemon
½ teaspoon ground ginger

Roll out the pastry and use to line a 20 cm (8 inch) ovenproof plate. Trim, knock up the edge and flute. Reserve the pastry trimmings. Prick the pastry base.

Sprinkle half the cornflakes or breadcrumbs in the pastry case and pour in the syrup. Sprinkle the lemon juice over the syrup.

Mix the ginger with the remaining cornflakes or breadcrumbs and sprinkle over the top. Cut strips from the pastry trimmings and make a lattice pattern over the tart.

Cook in a preheated moderately hot oven, 190°C (375°F), for 30 minutes until the pastry is crisp and golden. Serve hot or cold.
Serves 4

Orange Tart

1 × 225 g packet
  frozen shortcrust
  pastry, thawed
2 oranges, thinly
  sliced
1 egg, beaten
½ cup ground
  almonds
1 tablespoon sugar
2 tablespoons clear
  honey

Roll out the pastry and use to line a 20 cm (8 inch) flan dish. Prick the base. Line with a piece of greaseproof paper and dried beans. Bake blind in a preheated moderately hot oven, 190°C (375°F), for 15 minutes. Remove the beans and paper.

Meanwhile, put the oranges in a small pan. Add just enough water to cover and simmer for about 30 minutes until the peel is tender. Drain.

Beat together the egg, almonds and sugar until smooth. Spread in the flan case and arrange the orange slices on top. Spoon over the honey. Return to the oven for 20 minutes.

Serve hot or cold, with cream.
Serves 4

Stuffed Oranges

2 large oranges
1 dessert apple, peeled, cored and chopped
1 tablespoon raisins
1 tablespoon chopped dates
1 tablespoon hazelnuts, toasted and chopped
1 tablespoon brown sugar
½ cup cream
1 teaspoon icing sugar
orange twists to decorate (optional)

Halve the oranges and scoop out the flesh, keeping the shells intact; set aside.

Chop the orange flesh, discarding all pith, and place in a bowl. Add the apple, raisins, dates, nuts and brown sugar. Mix well and pile into the orange halves.

Whip the cream with the icing sugar until it forms soft peaks. Spoon on top of the oranges. Chill before serving, decorated with orange twists if liked.

Serves 4

Apple Toffee Dessert

1 medium cooking apple, peeled, cored and chopped
1 large dessert apple, peeled, cored and chopped
⅓ cup brown sugar
60 g (2 oz) butter
juice of ½ lemon
2 slices stale white bread, crusts removed, cut into cubes
4 tablespoons cream, lightly whipped

Sprinkle the apples with the sugar and toss well to coat evenly.

Melt half the butter in a frying pan, add the apple and fry quickly until just soft. Transfer to a warmed serving dish, using a slotted spoon. Sprinkle with the lemon juice and keep warm.

Melt the remaining butter in the pan, add the bread cubes and fry, turning, until crisp and evenly golden.

Add the bread to the apple pieces and mix well. Serve immediately, topped with whipped cream.

Serves 4

Citrus Trifles

4 wedges of sponge cake
2 tablespoons Cointreau
2 oranges
3 tablespoons lemon butter
2 egg whites
4 lemon twists to decorate

Cut the wedges in 3 and place in 4 individual glass dishes and sprinkle with the Cointreau.

Peel the oranges, removing all pith, and chop roughly. Divide between the dishes.

Put the lemon butter in a bowl. Whisk the egg whites until stiff and fold into the lemon butter. Spoon over the orange pieces.

Decorate with lemon twists. Chill before serving.
Serves 4

Chocolate Mousse

185 g (6 oz) dark chocolate, broken into pieces
3 tablespoons strong black coffee
1 tablespoon brandy
4 eggs, separated
TO DECORATE:
½ cup cream, whipped
flaked almonds, toasted

Put the chocolate, coffee and brandy in a bowl over a saucepan of hot water and stir until melted. Remove from the heat and leave to cool for 1 minute.

Add the egg yolks to the chocolate mixture and beat well. Whisk the egg whites until stiff and fold into the chocolate mixture.

Pour into a soufflé dish and chill for at least 3 hours before serving. Decorate with whipped cream and almonds.
Serves 4

Butterscotch Nut Pie

30 g (1 oz) butter
6 Nice biscuits,
  crushed
¾ cup milk
½ cup cream
1 × 50 g packet
  butterscotch quick
  mix
60 g (2 oz)
  hazelnuts, toasted
  and chopped
TO DECORATE:
½ cup cream,
  whipped
hazelnuts, toasted

Melt the butter and stir in the biscuit crumbs. Press into the base of a 15 cm (6 inch) flan dish.

Gradually add the milk and cream to the butterscotch mix, mixing until smooth. Add the hazelnuts and pile on top of the biscuit base.

Decorate with whipped cream and hazelnuts just before serving.
Serves 4

Pears en Compote

1 × 825 g can pear halves
1½ cups red wine
2 teaspoons ground cinnamon
⅓ cup dates, chopped

Drain the pears, reserving ¾ cup of the juice. Place the pears, wine, reserved pear juice and cinnamon in a pan. Bring to the boil, then lower the heat, cover and simmer for 10 minutes.

Add the dates, remove from the heat and leave to cool. Serve chilled, with cream if liked.

Serves 4-6

Baked Bananas

60 g (2 oz) butter
2 tablespoons brown sugar
2 tablespoons lemon juice
4 bananas
2 tablespoons brandy

Put the butter, sugar and lemon juice in a shallow casserole. Place in a preheated moderate oven, 180°C (350°F), for a few minutes until melted.

Cut the bananas into large pieces and arrange in the casserole, turning to coat with the sauce. Add the brandy, cover and return to the oven for 30 minutes.

Serve piping hot, accompanied by cream.

Serves 4

Ginger Rum Trifle

1 × 250 g (8 oz) ginger cake, sliced
1 × 225 g can pear quarters
4 tablespoons rum
1¼ cups cold thick custard
⅔ cup cream
1-2 teaspoons icing sugar
flaked almonds, toasted, to decorate

Line a medium soufflé dish or glass bowl with half the ginger cake.

Drain the pears, reserving 2 tablespoons of the juice. Mix the rum with the reserved pear juice and sprinkle half over the cake. Place the pears on top, cover with the remaining cake and pour over the remaining rum mixture.

Spoon the custard over the cake. Whip the cream with the icing sugar until it forms soft peaks. Spoon over the custard and decorate with almonds.

Serves 4

Caledonian Cream

3 tablespoons ginger marmalade
1 cup cream
3 tablespoons caster sugar
2 tablespoons whisky
2 tablespoons lemon juice
2 egg whites
brown sugar to decorate

Divide the marmalade between 4 individual glass dishes.

Whip the cream until stiff, then fold in the caster sugar, whisky and lemon juice. Whisk the egg whites until stiff and fold into the cream mixture.

Spoon the cream mixture over the marmalade and sprinkle with brown sugar to decorate.
Serves 4

Ginger Log

24 ginger snaps
3 tablespoons rum
2 cups cream
1½ teaspoons ground ginger
1 tablespoon caster sugar
1 tablespoon ginger syrup (from stem ginger)
stem ginger slices to decorate

Place the biscuits in a shallow dish and sprinkle with the rum. Leave until completely absorbed.

Whip the cream with the ground ginger and sugar until stiff. Fold in the ginger syrup.

Sandwich all the biscuits together, using two-thirds of the cream, to make a long roll. Place on a serving dish and cover with the remaining cream. Decorate with the stem ginger. Chill and serve.
Serves 4

Port and Prune Fool

1 cup cream
1 × 439 g can prunes, stoned
3 tablespoons port
⅓ cup brown sugar
grated nutmeg
chopped nuts to decorate

Whip the cream until stiff. Chop the prunes and fold into the cream with the port, sugar and nutmeg to taste.

Spoon into individual glass dishes and chill. Decorate with chopped nuts before serving.
Serves 4

Mont Blanc Meringues

½ cup cream
1 × 227 g can sweetened chestnut purée
2 tablespoons Grand Marnier
8 meringue nests
flaked almonds, toasted, to decorate

Whip the cream until stiff, then fold half into the chestnut purée with the Grand Marnier.

Pile the chestnut cream into the meringue nests. Swirl the remaining cream on top to resemble a snow-capped peak. Decorate with almonds. Serve immediately.
Serves 4

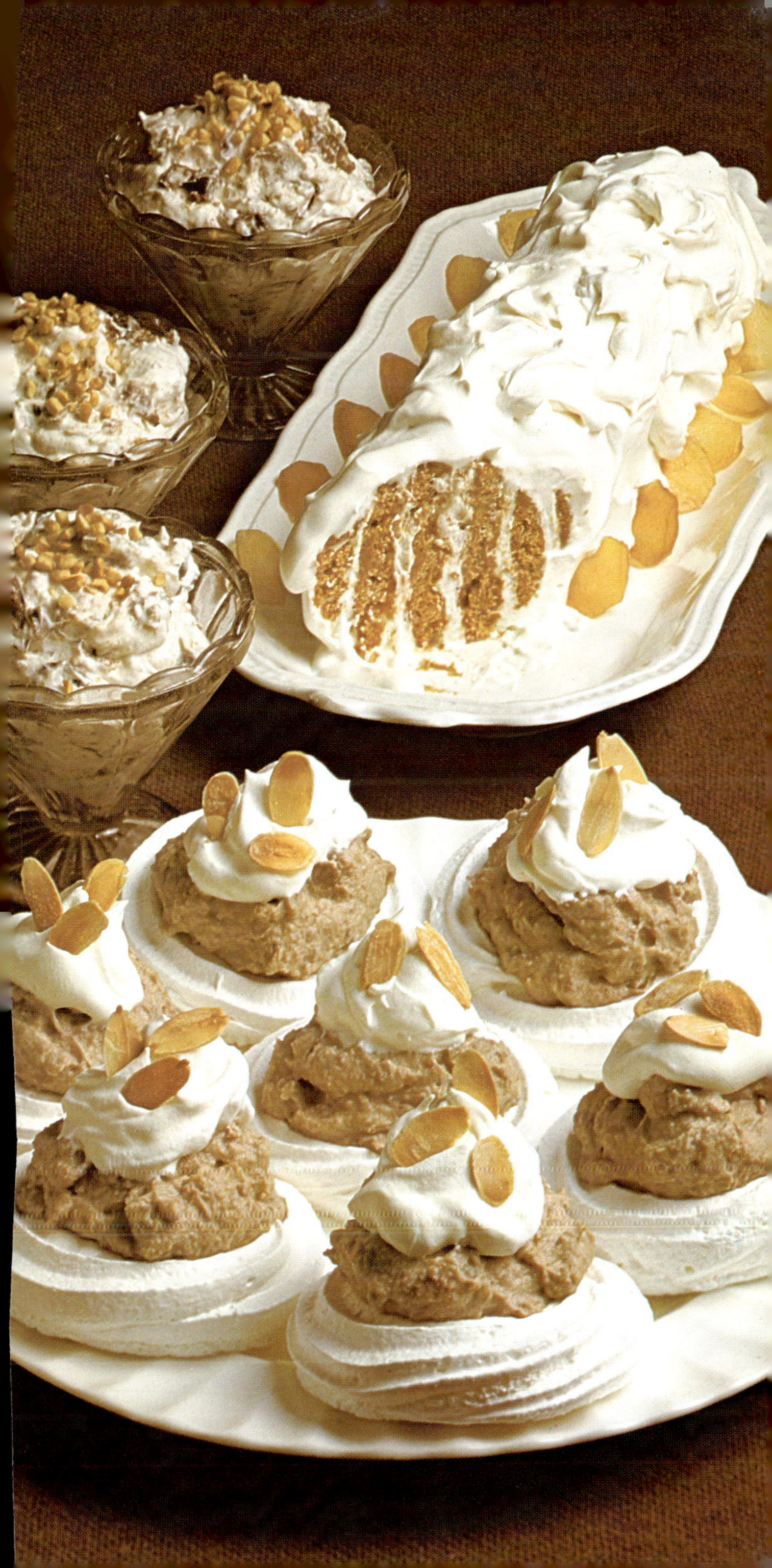

Iced Chocolate Mint Meringues

30 g (1 oz) dark chocolate, chopped
4 portions soft vanilla ice cream
8 meringue nests
3 tablespoons crème de menthe or Royal mint chocolate liqueur
grated chocolate to decorate (optional)

Fold the chocolate into the ice cream and spoon a portion into each meringue nest. Sprinkle the liqueur over the top. Decorate with grated chocolate if liked. Serve immediately.

Serves 4

NOTE: As a variation, use chopped peppermint chocolate instead of dark chocolate.

Puerto Rican Coffee Ice

1 × 225 g can peach slices, drained
3 tablespoons Tia Maria or Grand Marnier
⅓ cup sugar
2 tablespoons water
¼ cup flaked almonds, toasted
4 portions coffee ice cream

Divide the peach slices between 4 glass dishes, sprinkle with the liqueur and set aside.

Place the sugar and water in a small pan over low heat until dissolved, then boil steadily for 3 to 4 minutes until the syrup turns light brown. Immediately stir in the almonds and pour onto an oiled baking sheet. Leave to cool, then break the praline into pieces.

Place a portion of ice cream in each serving dish and top with the praline. Serve immediately.
Serves 4

INDEX

Apple:
  Apple toffee dessert 82
  Fried apple and cheese sandwiches 75
  Lamb and apple pie 30
  Liver and bacon with apple rings 34
Artichoke and bacon salad 18
Asparagus gratinée 23
Avocado with pears and black olives 19

Bacon:
  Braised cabbage with bacon 57
  French toasts with bacon 68
  Spinach with onion and bacon 50
  Artichoke heart and bacon salad 18
Bananas, baked 87
Barbecued lamb cutlets 31
Barbecued spare ribs 26
Beef:
  Beef and onion patties 72
  Chilli con carne 33
  London pie 32
  Roast beef salad with sour cream and olives 36
  Steak au poivre 35
Beetroot and orange salad 62
Brussels sprouts with chestnuts 57
Butterscotch nut pie 85

Cabbage:
  Braised cabbage with bacon 57
  Cabbage salad with peanut dressing 61
Caledonian cream 89
Carrot:
  Carrot and raisin salad 58
  Cream of carrot soup 8
  Herb-glazed carrots 52
Celery and onion soup 11
Celery with walnuts 51
Cheese:
  Baked cheese and mustard pudding 76
  English rarebit 66
  Fried apple and cheese sandwiches 75
  Mushroom and Emmenthal salad 15
  Potato and cheese pie 57
  Savoury macaroni cheese 71
  Tomato fondue 74
Chicken:
  Chicken with oranges and almonds 39
  Chicken and walnut pâté 16
  Chicken and walnut salad 41
  Pineapple chicken 40
  Spiced county chicken 38
Chilli con carne 33
Citrus trifles 83
Chocolate mint meringues, iced 92
Chocolate mousse 84
Corn bake, crispy 55
Corn fritters 54
Cucumber:
  Cucumber and prawn soup 11
  Prawn-stuffed cucumbers 22
Curried egg salad 65
Curry, seafood 42

Date and nut salad 63

Egg:
  Baked eggs in orange potatoes 77
  Curried egg salad 65
  Egg florentine 64
  Egg and onion casserole 67
  Eggs mimosa 21
  Fish and egg mornay 43
  Sardine eggs 15
  Smoked fish soufflé omelet 70
  Spanish omelet 70

Fish:
  Fish in caper mayonnaise 46
  Fish and egg mornay 43
  Fish and potato pie 44
  Fish in orange mayonnaise 49
  Smoked fish soufflé omelet 70
Frankfurter and bean hot pot 27
French toasts with bacon 68

Ginger log 90
Ginger rum trifle 88

Ham and mushroom toasts 73
Herb-glazed carrots 52

Lamb:
  Barbecued lamb cutlets 31
  Lamb and apple pie 30
  Liver and bacon with apple rings 34
  London pie 32

Macaroni cheese, savoury 71
Melon and anchovy salad 20
Mont Blanc meringues 90
Mushroom:
  Creamed mushrooms on toast 12
  Mushroom and Emmenthal salad 15
  Mushroom and onion casserole 52

Noodles, creamy herbed 66

Onion:
  Baked onions 52
  Mushroom and onion casserole 52
  Savoury onion puffs 74
Orange:
  Beetroot and orange salad 62
  Chicken with oranges and almonds 39
  Fish in orange mayonnaise 49
  Moroccan orange salad 79
  Orange tart 81
  Stuffed oranges 82

Pea and ham soup, cream of 8
Peanut dressing 61
Peanut soup, Georgian 7
Pears en compote 86
Pineapple chicken 40
Plums, pork fillet with 25
Pork:
  Barbecued spare ribs 26
  Pork chops with mustard sauce 24
  Pork fillet with plums 25
  Port and prune fool 90

Potato:
  Baked eggs in potatoes 77
  Fish and potato pie 44
  Potato and cheese pie 57
Prawn:
  Cucumber and prawn soup 11
  Prawn and artichoke vol-au-vents 46
  Prawn-stuffed cucumbers 22
Puerto Rican coffee ice 93

Salmon:
  Crunchy salmon salad 49
  Salmon savoury 69
Sardine eggs 15
Seafood curry 42
Smoked mackerel pâté 17
Spanish omelet 70
Spinach:
  Egg florentine 64
  Spinach consommé 6
  Spinach and cream cheese pâté 15
  Spinach with onion and bacon 50
Steak au poivre 35

Tomato:
  Roe-stuffed baked tomatoes 13
  Tomato fondue 74
  Tomato and yogurt soup 8
  Tomatoes with horseradish mayonnaise 59
Tongue, cold, giardinera 37
Treacle tart 80
Trout, baked 44
Tuna:
  Pacific tuna pie 45
  Tuna and bean salad 49

Veal:
  Tyrolean, with sour cream 28
  Veal stroganoff 29
Vegetable salad 60
Vichyssoise 11

Yogurt cheesecake 78

Acknowledgments

Recipes devised by Michelle Berriedale Johnson
Photograph by Melvin Grey